If you're interested in finding out more about our books, find us on Facebook at **Summersdale Publishers** and follow us on Twitter at **@Summersdale**.

www.summersdale.com

HOW TO SURVIVE UNIVERSITY

An Essential Pocket Guide

Tamsin King

Paperback   ISBN: 978 1 84953 890 9   £5.99

Tips and ideas from freshers'
week to final exams.

Whether your passion is society life, drinking shots or studying, your university experience will hold both new adventures and fresh challenges. This guide is packed with tips to help you survive and thrive at uni, from pulling an all-nighter in the library to an all-nighter at the club.

CONTENTS

INTRODUCTION

The decision to take a gap year is brave and sometimes scary. A year of freedom – it would be easy enough to spend it sleeping, but what can you do to make it worthwhile? How can you achieve something truly amazing and also have the time of your life? My friend, you have to make some plans…

Figuring out how to spend this year may be the biggest decision you've ever made. But whether you're getting workplace experience, learning through volunteering or immersing yourself in other cultures as you backpack around the world, the opportunities for fun and adventure this year are phenomenal. And you're bound to make friends along the way.

So you want to meet people from other cultures? See the wildlife from nature documentaries up close? Do you want to test yourself, learning new sports and skills? How to know where to start?

Here's where this little book will really help you out.

The choice of stuff out there to do is, frankly, bewildering. There are websites galore to explore. But this book is designed to get you thinking first about what you want – and to whet your appetite.

Most of these experiences are things that you would never have the chance to do at home. Others can be adapted to your budget. We've recommended certain locations around the world, but there's nothing stopping you from coming up with your own tailor-made adventures.

So go on, fire up your imagination and prepare to get out there…

SAFETY

Remember: your gap year should be exciting but, for everyone's sake, make sure you stay safe. Opt for reputable companies when you are choosing tour operators or activity schools – don't go with some Dodgy Dave just to save the price of a night out. Check if your insurance policy covers you – it won't cover every eventuality but it's

good to be forewarned. Test yourself but don't put yourself at risk: if you feel unsure about any aspect of your chosen activity, there's no harm in pulling out. Remember, one of the best things about your gap year adventures will be telling everyone at home later – so put your safety first and don't take unnecessary risks.

MONEY

You don't want to run out of dosh or be stranded somewhere and phoning home for help, so if you're not earning, you'll need to be somewhat budget-conscious. This book includes a range of activities, some of them dream trips but also plenty that won't deplete your funds too drastically. In many cases, the major expense is getting there, so plan your itinerary carefully. And with a little spin-doctoring you'll see how the life skills acquired while having these adventures may actually enhance your ability to make lots of loot later, so you can pay back everyone you've borrowed money from.

WILD THINGS

It's crazy but as we go about our ordinary lives in front of TVs and tablets, maybe with our beloved pooch or kitty close by, there are places where people see elephants on a daily basis. There are people whose actual job it is to take out boats to see whales leap out of the ocean. And if you've ever been up close to a big brute of an animal in the wild, then you certainly won't forget it. So take inspiration from the following ideas, get out there and see exactly what the natural world has to offer the gap year adventurer.

WHALE WATCHING

Gray whales migrate thousands of miles every year from Mexico to the Arctic, stopping off for a feed or two off Vancouver Island. So if you can make it to British Columbia, Canada, it would be just plain wrong to miss out on a sea safari to spot them and learn more about the marine ecosystem that includes several species of whales. Because there's nothing like seeing one of those vast beasties rising out of the ocean right beside you. The waters to the south and north of Vancouver Island are also home to the largest orca ('killer whale') population in the world. The best season to see whales is summer from late June through to September, when orca pods feed on the migrating salmon, and humpback and minke whales frequent the area. Most whales wisely head south again in the winter.

Four of the best whale-watching locations around the world:

★ **Monterey Bay, California** – year-round whale watching in the deep waters of the Monterey Submarine Canyon

★ **The Silver Bank in the Dominican Republic** – up to 5,000 humpbacks pass this spot from December to April each year

★ **Kaikoura, New Zealand** – a favourite haunt of sperm whales

★ **Western Cape, South Africa** – see up to 37 species, including southern right whales, breeding within visible distance of the coast from June to November

WILD WEST CATTLE DRIVES

Always fancied yourself in a Stetson, looking out over the lonesome plains? Love the notion of campfires and desert skies? Not afraid of a little heat and dust? From the days of the American Wild West, cowboys drove herds of cattle between winter and summer pastures, for branding or to take them to market, and ranches now invite paying guests to be part of it. Look for an authentic experience and take your riding skills to a new level as you join a cattle drive through the magnificent mountain ranges and craggy canyons of North America, or for something even more different consider a cattle drive in rural Argentina with the gauchos. Alternatively, a longer stint in the raw, powerful landscape of the Australian outback is a favourite for gap years as some schemes will even allow you to pay your way with farm work.

SWIMMING WITH DOLPHINS

Few people are left unchanged by an encounter with a dolphin in the wild. In the spectacular setting of Drake Bay on the Osa Peninsula in Costa Rica – teeming with marine life including whales, manta rays and sea turtles – you can swim with wild dolphins in crystal-clear warm waters and witness how they behave in their natural environment. Combine your stay with rainforest tours in Corcovado National Park – one of the most 'biologically intense' places on Earth. There are centres offering tours in dolphin-frequented waters around the world, from Ireland and Portugal to Florida and New Zealand (eco-friendly outfits can't guarantee the wild creatures will show up, but they should tell you the likely success rate). Opting to go with one of the many well-established conservation groups that organise tours means that your money goes towards the preservation of this beautiful species.

AFRICAN BUSH WALKING

Step out of the vehicle... and into the most intense wildlife experience in Africa. Connecting with the wild on foot is the interactive alternative to the typical Land-Rover safari, and it allows you to take in the sounds and smells and even tastes of the bush up close and personal while reducing your impact on the environment. Qualified local guides teach you about tracking animals and survival skills, and you'll be able to take stunning, close-up photos and maybe visit out-of-the-way caves with ancient rock art. Bush walking either for a day or extended camping tour is the way to get a deeper understanding of African wildlife and its environment, and the experience is offered in many of Africa's National Game Parks (never attempt to go without a guide, obviously). What would you do if you found a snake in your path? There's one way to find out.

But where in Africa? Experts recommend:

★ **Botswana** – Northern Tuli Game Reserve or Selinda Reserve

★ **Zambia** – South Luangwa National Park, where the walking safari was pioneered

★ **Zimbabwe** – Mana Pools or Hwange National Park

★ **South Africa** – Kruger National Park

★ **Kenya** – Matthews Mountain Range Forest or Naboisho Conservancy

HORSE TREKKING

How about exploring the route of the famous Bear's Ring Trail in Finland on the back of a sturdy Finnish horse? Just below the Arctic Circle are some of Europe's oldest forests and pure, remote wilderness, where you can learn about southern Lapland's Sami people, their myths and equine traditions. As you make your way through rugged scenery you camp at cosy log cabins and relax after a day in the saddle in a steaming sauna. Treks leave from May to October when temperatures are warmer, and during the long hours of daylight you may be lucky enough to spot reindeer and elk (tip: in September, most of the biting insects are gone). For a gentler introduction, try a half-day trek through the foothills of the Atlas Mountains in Morocco. Or for the experienced, why not take the ultimate horse trek across the wild and weather-beaten steppes of Mongolia?

WATCHING ORANGUTANS

The 'red man of the forest' once roamed freely across most of South-East Asia, but due to deforestation for farming they are now restricted to the islands of Borneo and Sumatra. Situated near to Sandakan, known as the gateway to Borneo's wildlife, the Sepilok Nature Reserve has a sanctuary for illegally captured, orphaned or injured orangutans to be taught to survive in the wild. Volunteer placements are available, so if you have a passion for the eco-friendly and what's off-the-beaten track, this may be for you. Marvel at the prowess and grace of the wild orangutans of northern Borneo as they swing through the trees and fix you with one of their famous soulful gazes. Borneo's national parks are also home to pygmy elephants and proboscis monkeys. You can stay in a rustic bungalow, and maybe awake to find an orangutan or a pig-tail macaque chilling out on your veranda.

MEET MOUNTAIN GORILLAS

Gorilla safaris promise a mind-blowing encounter beyond any other wildlife experience. Trekking to an altitude of 2,500 metres on steep, muddy paths through the dense forest and tightly-knit vines, you emerge into a clearing and come face to face with a 200-kilo silverback gorilla just a stone's throw away. In a story made famous by the film *Gorillas in the Mist*, Dian Fossey dedicated her life to these elusive great apes, one of our closest primate relatives. It's now much safer to visit their green oasis hidden away in the mountains of East Africa, but it's a fragile ecosystem that is home to the few surviving in the wild. Ten groups are habituated to humans, and sitting just metres away from a mountain gorilla is one of the most exclusive wildlife adventures. Guided tours take place in Mgahinga National Park in Uganda and Virunga Volcanoes National Park in Rwanda.

AN ETHICAL ELEPHANT EXPERIENCE

Thinking of seeing Thailand from the swaying back of a mighty Indian elephant? Well, think again, and consider a visit to an elephant sanctuary instead. *Lonely Planet* says there is now overwhelming evidence that riding elephants is harmful to them. On the other hand, Elephant Nature Park in Chiang Mai, a non-profit organisation and the best known of a handful of such refuges, cares for elephants mistreated by irresponsible tourism and logging industry practices. You can feed them fresh fruit, watch them take their morning bath – ridding themselves of their self-applied insect repellent of mud – and also walk with them. Getting a much better sense of how the endangered Asian elephants act together in groups in the wild, you could even look into a volunteer placement.

GREAT WHITE SHARK DIVING

If the idea of diving in shark-infested waters and getting up close and personal with one of the most terrifying predators on the planet gives you a thrill, then Dyer Island off the coast of Cape Town is the place for you. This island is the Great White capital of the world thanks to its copious population of seals, which makes it an ideal feeding ground. Cage dive in the aptly named 'shark alley' and come face to face with the rock stars of the ocean. Not for the faint hearted. Visibility is best from March to September, and always ensure that your chosen operator uses ethical practices – sharks have feelings too (and they can injure themselves when attacking a cage). If you prefer some toughened glass between you and Jaws, try an 'aqua sub' in South Australia instead.

WATCHING THE WILDEBEEST

Let's be honest, if sharks are rock stars, wildebeest are… roadies, perhaps. Actually they look a little like roadies – hefty creatures with interesting facial hair. But here's the thing: every year up to 1.5 million wildebeest, zebra and gazelle migrate across the African plains to congregate on the feeding grounds in the Masai Mara. And even *National Geographic*, who know a thing or two, say it's one of the greatest wildlife spectacles on Earth. If you are in Kenya, you could be lucky enough to witness it, staying in a lodge or campsite and taking a locally arranged safari to get a real piece of the action. Wildebeest herds constantly search for fresh grass and water. From December to March you can watch them in Serengeti National Park. In April and May they head along the Western Corridor to Lake Victoria before migrating to the Masai Mara.

ANIMAL WELFARE

If you want to do something practical to help the survival of species considered endangered, you could adopt or sponsor an animal for the cost of a sandwich every month, and you'll receive a photo as well as regular updates on how your adopted animal and their environment are being protected. Among the most endangered species are the hawksbill turtle, the giant panda, the golden lion tamarin, the black rhino, the snow leopard, the orangutan and the mountain gorilla. Why not adopt an animal, then make a plan to visit them during your gap year? Animal-lovers can also have awesome adventures in Ecuador by working with rescued wildlife while staying in the Amazon jungle. When considering a wildlife adventure, responsible tourism websites such as www.travel4wildlife.com have tips on where to go and what to do.

AQUATIC ADVENTURES

Self-confessed water babies, look no further. If you are never happier than when you're splashing about in the waves, then spend more time at sea on your gap year. There is nothing more guaranteed to put a smile on your face, get you fit and make you feel more at one with the universe – we're about 60 per cent water, after all. Maybe it's time to conquer your fear of the deep or learn to surf? If you get bored lounging on a beach and prefer to be active there are plenty of water sports to keep you entertained.

IN THE DEEP

Imagine gliding effortlessly through crystal clear waters, surrounded by tropical fish and coral in all the colours of the spectrum. Many diving centres offer guided dives for beginners with experienced instructors. But this might be the time to gain a PADI diving qualification – then the underwater world will be your oyster from Malaysia to Mexico. Australia's Great Barrier Reef, the longest-spanning natural wonder in the

world, also happens to be one of the cheapest and most popular places to learn – Australian dive facilities from Rottnest Island in Western Australia to Lord Howe Island off New South Wales have a reputation for high standards and quality gear. If you have time to spare, which is what a gap year is all about, then consider a programme where you assist in marine conservation – if you wouldn't mind living on a beach in Fiji, or collecting information about one of the Indian Ocean's most extensive and beautiful coral reefs in Madagascar.

SNORKELLING

Snorkel yourself happy... This relaxed, water-based activity is a great way to keep fit and healthy and gain a sense of peace and calm, exploring the seas in a more casual way. It's even said to be good for boosting your creativity. The KwaZulu-Natal coast of South Africa offers excellent snorkelling among stunning reefs and shipwrecks. If you're apprehensive of jumping from a boat into deep water, don't worry. Some tours will take you to sandy coves or islands where you can enter the water from the beach, and many companies offer float coats for extra buoyancy, so all you have to do is kick and gaze. Visibility is best in the South African winter. Other great snorkelling destinations include Thailand's Similan Marine Park and Barbados, where in the clear waters you can see turtles, manta rays and barracudas.

RAFTING

Where 'mosi-o-tunya' or 'the smoke that thunders' pounds the waters of the mighty Zambezi into a violent froth at the foot of Victoria Falls, you can get into a raft with eight other people and hurtle downstream along the churning rapids. This ultimate white-water rafting destination has some of the world's best instructors and support teams, amid some of the best scenery in Africa. It's a good idea to have some canoeing or white-water experience; while it's not usually required, you'll probably get more out of the ride. Another top place for a raft trip experience is the Grand Canyon. Multi-day adventures let you camp along the river while escorted by guides in the National Park. This can sometimes involve a helicopter in or out, or a night at a working cattle ranch on the rim of the canyon.

PADDLE YOUR OWN CANOE

To paddle your own canoe means to act independently and decide your own destiny – which is what gap year adventures are all about, when you think about it. But you can take it literally too, and propel your own pointy narrow water-going craft. Do it in the place they do it best – the wilds of Canada. Head up to the Northwest Territories and take a trip around Yellowknife's crystal clear waters, smooth rock shorelines and tree-fringed lakes, catching fish for dinner. Or explore the lakes of Ontario's Algonquin Park, looking out for moose and listening for wolves, staying at a log cabin.

Wherever you are, being in a canoe means you won't have to worry about leeches, snakes or spiders, leaving you free to spot wildlife. It helps you reach places you can't reach with your feet

or a vehicle, whether around a steep coastline or through thick jungle. The mangroves, sea caves, towering canyons and serene lagoons in Thailand are exceptional, and sea canoe trips at Phang Nga Bay let you paddle among the sheer limestone cliffs jutting vertically out of emerald green water – you'll escape the crowds and find quiet beaches.

A kayak is like a canoe but enclosed – useful for challenging white-water rivers – and propelled using a two-ended paddle. For action-packed kayaking, try the rainforest of the Amazon basin, where white-water rivers drain straight out of the Andes, or in Costa Rica, you can kayak through the canals of Tortuguero, where paddling quietly through the calm waters allows you to observe the forest canopy on the lookout for monkeys and sloths. In the Camargue region of the south of France you can kayak the lagoons among wild horses and flocks of flamingos.

JET-SKIING

If you like a bit of vroom in your adventure, this is an exciting and high-speed way to explore a coastline, and there aren't many more beautiful places to try it than Greece, where you can hop from deserted island to hidden cove with the wind in your hair, explore a few caves and be back in time for cocktails. On Santorini, one of the most spectacular Greek islands, roar across the deep blue waters to the volcano and stop to do some snorkelling. Be ready for a pure adrenalin rush. When you're out skimming across the waves, be sure to slow down when you take corners; if you come off and hit the water at high speed it can really hurt! And use the jet-ski for exploring coastline that can't be reached from land – not for annoying people on the beach.

SAIL AWAY

Sailing is social, it tests your stamina and you're up against the elements. Crewing means standing watch through the night, hoisting sails, and expanding a whole range of practical skills. You learn about leadership and teamwork, and discover strengths you didn't know you had. You also have unparalleled access to dramatic sunsets and sunrises, dolphins and laughter, and nothing can compare with the thrill of discovering an uninhabited island to explore. The perfect location to hire a sailing boat or go out on a guided sailing tour is the Caribbean, where you can jump on a catamaran and cruise gracefully around all day, and some companies take on temporary crews to work on their yachts as they move between islands. You could work as anything from a deck hand to a cook depending on your skills if you have some basic sailing experience.

GO JUMP OFF A CLIFF...

The concept is simple: find a cliff and jump or dive off it into the water. It is, however, a great way to challenge yourself with a short, sharp burst of terror and exhilaration. As extreme sports go, it's uncomplicated, but if you think about leaping from the equivalent of a rather tall building in just your swimmers then you'll want to make that touchdown as perfect as can be. You really don't want to think about the consequences otherwise. So this sport is only recommended if you learn to do it properly. In South Africa's Kamikaze Kanyon, where the pastime is also known as Kloofing, you can jump from heights of 3 to 22 metres into sparkling and inviting rock pools. But please don't try this anywhere without proper guidance and an awareness of the risks involved.

SURFING

Do you dream of learning to surf – that first moment when you glide down the waves? Riding a surfboard brings a feeling of freedom like no other. Beginner courses are designed to be great fun and get you up on your board and enjoying the surf as soon as possible. Australian companies offer week-long surf camps between Sydney and Byron Bay especially for gap year travellers, so you can meet likeminded people as you ride the waves on some of Australia's most beautiful beaches. If you're a surfer looking for a challenge, test your skills at these top locations:

★ Virgin reef-breaks in the Outer Orkneys

★ Wild waves in Sri Lanka

★ The Cloudbreak, Wilkes, Swimming Pools, Desperations and Lighthouse breaks in Fiji

★ Temple point-breaks in Indonesia

★ The ultimate break – the right-hand point at Jeffreys Bay, South Africa

WINDSURFING

Dahab, on the Sinai peninsula of Egypt, is a laid-back resort on the edge of a desert landscape. Looking out over the Gulf of Aqaba, the surrounding scenery is spectacular, with impressive mountains forming a dramatic backdrop to the shimmering blue sea. The wind record is another good reason to head here for windsurfing: it boasts around 300 days a year of force 4 to 7 winds. There is flat water stretching far out to sea from the beach, protected from the gulf by a sandbank making it perfect for getting to grips with the basics. Dahab attracts a younger crowd and is a well-known area for diving. Make the most of your stay by enjoying Bedouin hospitality in the desert under the stars.

KITE SURFING

A fusion of wakeboarding, surfing, windsurfing and kite flying, kitesurfing or kiteboarding is the wildest water sport around. To be sure of finding the right conditions, head to Cape Hatteras, North Carolina, recognised as one of the world's top locations – the cape is only a mile wide and juts out 30 miles from the mainland, allowing for spectacular sunrises and sunsets. Margarita Island, just off the northern Venezuelan coast, benefits from a reliable wind from November to June and only a stone's throw away is the island of Coche, which has its very own kiteboarding speed track along the beach edge, created by offshore winds blowing across the salt flats. As you pick up the basics, you'll learn the skill of visually assessing the strength and direction of the wind, giving you an enormous sense of being in touch with the elements.

SPEND A YEAR DOING THE SPORT YOU LOVE

Already an experienced windsurfer, surfer or diver? You could train as an instructor in order to travel and earn money from the sport you love. Beyond the technical and safety knowledge, you'd also develop your communication and motivational skills – very helpful for your CV. And in the meantime you spend month after month on the water – perhaps living in Thailand, Mexico or Greece for free.

CULTURAL ADVENTURES

Gap years don't have to be all adrenalin, thrills and spills. There are countless opportunities to expand your mental and cultural horizons too. If you're heading abroad, you'll come into contact with rich and fascinating cultures, perhaps ancient traditions, and a rewarding experience can come from doing something as simple as trying things the way the locals do it. In fact, you can make cultural exploration the focus of your whole trip.

CUISINES AND CULTURES

One way to dig below the surface of a culture is to understand its food. If you're planning to spend several months abroad, you'd better learn how to use those strange foodstuffs you find in the shops. And how popular will you be if you go home knowing how to knock up a Thai curry from scratch? The Chiang Mai Kitchen Cooking School provides all the fresh ingredients you will need from their own herb and vegetable garden and the local market, and will instruct you in how to prepare delicious and authentic Thai meals like prawn and coconut milk soup, papaya salad and jungle curry. There are cooking courses for foreigners in many cities around the world, so whether you want to make kimchi in Korea or Mexican food in Oaxaca, there's a chef's hat with your name on it…

OPEN-AIR OPERA

Where better to get your first taste of the opera than in the fully functioning open-air Roman arena in Verona, home of Romeo and Juliet? With superb sets and a history of renowned opera singers (both Maria Callas and Luciano Pavarotti performed here), this really is opera as it should be – especially when over 20,000 people, each with a lighted candle, eagerly await the opening lines of *Aida* on a balmy August evening. Marvel at the elegant upper class of Verona and pop into one of the traditional Italian *gelaterie* in the main square for an ice cream. Do resist the temptation to start singing 'Just one cornetto…' If your passion for culture is stoked by this, you could also spend an evening watching a ballet in the Roman amphitheatre down the road.

LEARN TO TANGO

It takes more than two lessons to tango, it's true, but it's not too late to give it a try... Argentinians are famous for their passionate natures and they pour this passion into tango, surely one of the sexiest forms of dance, which originated in Buenos Aires in the nineteenth century. Are you up to the challenge? The true tango masters take years to perfect their skills – tango isn't just a dance in Argentina; it's an expression of their cultural heritage. If you want to try out your moves, go along to a *milonga* at one of the many famous clubs in Buenos Aires, where sometimes world professionals perform as guests. In San Telmo, locals tango throughout the day at the Sunday market in Plaza Dorrego and there are sometimes free lessons late in the day. Tango Buenos Aires Festival takes place in August.

THE ART OF CAPOEIRA

Capoeira is an ancient Afro-Brazilian fusion of dance and martial art, first practised by African slaves who were brought to Brazil over 400 years ago. Forbidden from practising any martial art, they developed this discipline in which dance-like movements focus on energy release and body control, disguising its combative qualities. Set to the rhythm of voices and drums, capoeira is arguably as popular as football in northern Brazil and is now an international art form combining athleticism, acrobatics, culture and creativity. Learn all about this unique art and tap into a whole new philosophy of movement in the state of Bahia, where you can take capoeira lessons on the beach at sunrise.

MEET INDIGENOUS AUSTRALIANS

For 40,000 years the Arrernte Aboriginal tribal group has met at Alice Springs in Central Australia to trade art and knowledge. Today you can visit the site and meet Aboriginal artists, learn about the 'dreamtime' stories associated with their art and take lessons in playing the didgeridoo – considered one of the oldest musical instruments on Earth, designed to conjure the sounds of nature. Find out about the spiritual-physical relationships in aboriginal life, look for 'bush tucker' (and have a taste) and see demonstrations of music and dance. The Aboriginal Australia Art and Culture Centre is 100 per cent Aboriginal owned and operated, which means you're not only learning about their traditions but meeting the people and contributing to keeping their culture alive.

GET STEAMY IN HUNGARY

Budapest is the only large city in the world with 80 geothermal springs and its ornate bathing places are duly famous, yet a spa experience can be had for very little money. Visit Hungary's 'Spa City' to refresh your weary backpacking limbs in the healing mineral waters. Some of the thermal springs have been known for two thousand years, while the Art Nouveau Gellért Spa is within a World Heritage site, so soak up the atmosphere and history, bathing as the Ottomans and Romans did. You can indulge in a massage, laze about in a steam room, or (at St Lucas Medicinal Bath and Swimming Pool) flop into the hot-water mud pool. Many of the bath houses offer 'women only' or 'men only' days, so check the timetables before you go.

DOG-SLEDDING

Tearing along the ice on a toboggan behind a team of huskies is an exhilarating adventure to get your heart racing and your blood pumping. In Norway, the 'Land of the Midnight Sun', you can sit back and enjoy the ride with your own personal driver, or take the reins and drive a team of six dogs. The real thrill comes from being in control yet always feeling that you are on the edge of losing your grip or careering off wildly across the ice. This is an addictive way to travel so you may be inspired to sign up for a longer trip deep into the silent, snowy wilderness. If you choose to go in the near darkness of the Arctic winter the weather conditions will be harsh, but this is the best time of year to see the spectacular Northern Lights.

EAT FUGU

Unless you're from Japan or Korea (or just not a very good cook), the chances are you're not yet acquainted with the cultural experience that is dicing with death at dinner. For a culinary adventure out of the ordinary, take a bite out of the delicious yet deadly poisonous puffer fish, known as fugu, whose toxins have the power to instantly paralyse and kill you. A mere 200 people or less are poisoned through eating incorrectly prepared fugu each year! Only dare to try this delicacy in restaurants in Japan and Korea that hold official fugu licences. The most affordable place is in Osaka, but apparently the tastiest fugu come from Korea and it's at its most appetising if caught between October and March. If fugu sounds too frightening, challenge your palate in Korea with sea cucumbers and the freshest sushi you've ever picked out of the tank.

THE FOOTSTEPS OF ARTISTS

Immerse yourself in the world that inspired your favourite artist by taking a walking or cycling tour through their landscape, and discover a whole new dimension to their work. The Provence region of France inspired many of Van Gogh's most famous paintings so you could start at Arles, sipping a glass of wine on the famous terrace featured in *Café de Nuit*. Carry on through the Camargue towards Saintes-Maries-de-la-Mer to see the beach where he painted *Fishing Boats on the Beach*. From here, head to Eygalières on the lookout for a *Wheat Field with Cypresses* and then hike through Les Alpilles, the 'Little Alps', making your final stop at St Paul de Mausole, the twelfth-century monastery where he painted *Starry Night Over the Rhone*. That's just an example – pick your own favourite artist or writer, plan an itinerary, and don't forget to pack your own sketchpad or notebook.

APPRECIATE THE ANCIENT INCAS

The ruins of Machu Picchu above the Sacred Valley of south-eastern Peru are an awe-inspiring sight, with distant views of the snow-capped Cordillera Vilcabamba and the deep green valley below. The air of mystery surrounding the mist-shrouded terraces of this fifteenth-century Inca site is what makes this an unforgettable cultural adventure. The 26-mile Inca Trail is world-famous, though a challenge with steep climbs and cold temperatures, so it usually takes four days. You need to book months in advance and don't plan to hike before you've acclimatised to the altitude, unless you want to get sick, so perhaps spend some time learning about the fascinating Inca civilisation before you set out. If you time it right, you can arrive at dawn to see the sun rise over the citadel of Machu Picchu before anyone else arrives.

PEAK
EXPERIENCES

Whether you enjoy climbing up mountains or jumping off them, if you've got loads of energy and a desire to see things from the best possible view, there's something in this section for you. Be aware of the risks of physical exercise at high altitudes and, as with any of the adventures in this book, look before you leap and read up in advance on any potential hazards in areas you plan to tackle. Take it to the level that you feel comfortable with, but the sky's the limit.

MOUNTAIN BIKING IN CORSICA

With its inland peaks, Mediterranean sun, light breezes and rugged coastline dotted with ancient villages, Corsica is the ideal place for a mountain-biking adventure. Experience the thrill of plunging down mountain tracks or winding your way up through mountain passes and along the imposing clifftop coastal routes. You could explore the wind-buffeted Cap Corse of the north, the 2,697-metre snow-topped Mount Cinto or the unusual rock formations known as 'calanques' along the coast from Ajaccio to Porto, inhaling the scent of wild, flowering maquis shrubs. Most trails are free to access, but you will need to hire equipment unless you take it with you. Other extreme biking trails you should check out are the 1,000 Steps in Ferntree Gully, Melbourne and the Colorado Trail, extending from Denver to Durango.

ROCK CLIMBING

The ultimate challenge of strength and technique, climbing is one of the hardest and most rewarding physical activities. It's also a sport that you can do almost anywhere in the world, admiring spectacular scenery as you climb your way to a vantage point. You don't need previous experience, as most climbing centres or tour operators will offer lessons for beginners, but it is vital to have a guide and the right equipment. One of the best locations in Europe is the Vercors region near Grenoble in France. This rugged and

magnificent landscape, which sits in the shadow of the Alps, is infused with the history of the resistance fighting during the Second World War and offers routes for all levels of ability. Other great spots for rock climbing in Europe include El Chorro near Malaga in southern Spain and the island of Kalymnos in Greece. Experienced climbers looking for new challenges could try the Atlas Mountains in Morocco, an area full of unexplored rock faces where you can bag yourself a few 'first ascents'. For an icy challenge, look to Norway. And if you're in upstate New York, a must are the Shawangunks, better known as the Gunks, in the Adirondack Mountains.

VIA FERRATA

Fancy rock climbing without risks and ropes? Then take an 'iron way', or *via ferrata*. These routes created from metal cables, steps, bridges and ladders guide those with less experience of climbing to get high up on sheer rock faces and enjoy jaw-dropping views while secured to a steel cable. They're mostly purpose-built for outdoor challenges and thrills, but in Italy's Dolomites they originated during the First World War, built by the *Alpini* troops for access over the mountainous terrain. If you take a multi-day trip here you can sleep in mountain huts and will see wartime trenches along the way. The world's highest is on Mount Kenya in East Africa, an extinct volcano with plenty of ridges and peaks as well as receding glaciers; the national park around it is home to elephants, rhinos and leopards. Iceland has one too at Coldback Mountain, overlooking a fjord.

ALBANIAN 'ALPS' ADVENTURE

A century ago, explorer Edith Durham said she forgot all about the rest of the world in the 'accursed mountains' or Dinaric Alps of Albania, and not much has changed. Boar, lynx and wolves still roam in these mountains north of Greece, which are still well off the beaten track and offer thrilling adventures on a cheap budget. Thethi National Park is remote and magnificent, and parts of the mountains are virtually impenetrable. Traditional wooden houses have 'lock-in' towers to shelter the men in times of blood feud and you can trek with mules across the Valbona Pass, eating traditional food. Take the ferry out of the mountains through the fjord-like Lake Koman, then spend a few days enjoying the nightlife of Tirana or the beaches in the south.

ABSEILING

Going down? Abseiling enthusiasts will tell you that the greatest rush is actually in the *descent* of a mountain. Rappelling was once what you did after climbing a cliff to get back down, but abseiling down a giant wall of rock is now seen as a sport in itself. You'll be taking the more exciting and direct route back to base camp as you dangle from the edge of a cliff on a rope. And 'controlled descent', as it's also known, doesn't take long to learn. Get to know the ropes in the UK in North Wales, the Peak District or Cumbria; experience a rush of adrenalin just looking at pictures of the sheer and gut-wrenchingly tall Gordon Dam, surrounded by wilderness in Tasmania.

Other top jaw-dropping locations include:

★ **New Zealand**, where you can abseil down waterfalls in Egmont National Park or into a 'Lost World' cavern underground

★ **South Africa**, from the dizzying heights of Cape Town's spectacular Table Mountain, step off the edge of the 1,000-metre landmark into oblivion, but don't forget to look around and take in the astounding views of the Atlantic below

TREK MOUNT KILIMANJARO

Hike your way up 5,895 metres to The Roof of Africa. You'll get fitter, take fantastic photos and see volcanic craters and high-altitude tundra in tropical Africa. A once-active volcano, the snow-capped Mount Kilimanjaro rises abruptly from Tanzania's north-east plains and is the world's highest free-standing mountain whose summit can be reached by walking. Your ascent will take you through farmlands, lush rainforest teeming with elephants, buffaloes, rhinos, leopards and monkeys, and finally across a barren lunar landscape to the twin summits. Hiking tours last from five to seven days, depending on which route you take. You must have a good level of fitness and it is essential that you go with a guide. The sense of achievement is priceless.

WINTER IN THE MOUNTAINS

Imagine waking up to clean air and the sun glinting off the snow every morning. If the notion of strapping on skis every day is worth working for, then sign up for a season in the mountains. Skiing or snowboarding can be an expensive way to amuse yourself on a tightly budgeted gap year, but if you train as a ski or snowboard instructor, or work in a resort kitchen or as a chalet host, in return you'll have free and unlimited access to the slopes. If this sounds like a perfect way to earn as you travel, sign up for a season at the Rocky Mountains in Canada; or if you're already in the southern hemisphere, the ski season in the Chilean Andes runs from June to September, the resorts are much smaller than Europe, and you are never far from stunning tropical scenery or the beach.

HELI HIKING ON A GLACIER

Want to do something you will definitely be writing home about? Heli hiking is just a little bit special. They say it's a once in a lifetime experience but I dunno, I think I'd want to go again. A helicopter picks you up and whisks you away over a jaw-dropping landscape – let's say the Franz Josef Glacier on New Zealand's South Island, because it's so stunning. (Go on. Google it.) A guide helps you traverse the glacier safely and make the most of your time in this pristine, frozen blue kingdom, with its maze of ice caves and tunnels and glistening ice pinnacles – a bizarre contrast

with the temperate rainforest below. Glacier equipment and walking axes usually come included in the tour – just remember to wrap up warm and do not forget your camera. Heli hiking can be pricey but it's definitely worth it for the chance to walk in terrain that's impossible to reach by any other means. Another top location for heli hiking is the Rocky Mountains in Canada. If you're on a tight budget, day tours will take you to more accessible regions of these glaciers on foot – just brace yourself for a climb. In Iceland, glacier hiking and ice caving tours are on offer all year round. With crampons on your hiking boots, you'll be surrounded by thousand-year-old ice in a majestic landscape that is totally humbling and you can't help but marvel at the power of nature.

VOLCANO WALKING

Watch spectacular volcanic activity up close and you'll get an amazing sense of the powerful geological forces that created the Earth's surface and are still shaping it. This is mountaineering with a difference. Guatemala has the highest density of active volcanoes anywhere on the planet, with Pacaya, Fuego and Santiaguito all within 200 km of each other; the country also has colourful villages, Mayan markets and warm and friendly people. Home of Pele the Hawaiian volcano goddess, Hawaii Volcano National Park on Big Island is also a fantastic place to try volcano walking. Climb Haleakala, the world's largest dormant volcano, and admire its bizarre moonscape, or marvel as lava spews out of Thurston Lava Tube into the sea. Another great location is northern Sulawesi, Indonesia. You can tackle some volcano trails alone, but to get the most out of your trek it's best to go with a guide.

TRAINS, CAMELS AND AUTOMOBILES

There's a bit of the explorer in each of us, and so many different ways of seeing the world. Instead of simply flying to a destination, think about other modes of travel. Whether you'd prefer to travel under your own steam or set out on the mother of all road trips, the journey is as important as the destination – so let these ideas fuel your sense of adventure.

TRANS-SIBERIAN RAILWAY

If you're heading to Asia for your gap year, you could start your journey in Moscow and take the longest train journey in the world: 9,288 km to Vladivostok. Alternatively there's the 7,867-km Trans-Mongolian route from Moscow to Beijing via Ulan-Bator and the Gobi desert. The railway, built between 1891 and 1916, passes the Ural Mountains and Lake Baikal; travel in summer for the most daylight. Do the seven-day journey all in one go or stop off in Russia and Mongolia on the way. Train expert 'The Man in Seat 61' (see his website for more details) says the Vladivostok route is less of an international travellers' train and more a locals' train, so it's a more interesting travel experience – one where you're more likely to meet Russians. It's also clean, comfortable and safe, and it stops from time to time so you can get out and take photographs.

HOSTEL HOPPING

Meandering from one hostel to another at your own leisurely pace is a great way to explore your chosen destination, and door-to-door backpacking buses now operate in many of the popular backpacking regions. Jump on the Baz Bus in South Africa and take a tour from Cape Town or Johannesburg, stopping off at hostels when, where, and for as long as you like, all with one hassle-free ticket. The only rule is that you have to keep travelling in the same direction. The tickets don't have an expiry date, but you will need to purchase a return ticket if you want to end your journey back at the city you started off in. Staying in a hostel helps you meet like-minded travellers and get ideas of things to do, and if you join Hostelling International up front there are often discounts.

ON YOUR BIKE

If you're already acquainted with the joys of cycle-touring, then you know that an adventure can be had anywhere – just sling a compass and map into your backpack, pack lightly and get on the road. But don't worry about donning the lycra: cycling is simply a great way to explore, giving you the freedom and flexibility to cover more ground than you could on foot while slowing down whenever you want. You could try island cycling in France: go to one of the many islands off the French coast such as L'île d'Ouessant in Brittany, and hire a bike for the day. You can get an enormous sense of achievement by cycling

the whole way around the island, stopping off wherever takes your fancy.

In Vietnam, get away from the bustling cities and see the countryside by joining the locals on their favourite form of transport – the bicycle. For an easy ride, head to the flatlands of the Mekong Delta, where you pass rice paddies and little villages. If you're feeling more adventurous, tackle the hills surrounding Hanoi, or even travel the historical Ho Chi Minh trail. This way of touring the country will cost you little more than the price of hiring a bicycle (although booking an organised trip can be fun) and it's an excellent way of getting to know the friendly and welcoming local people. A cycle tour will get you fit and take you into the heart and soul of the country.

ON THE ROAD

Some places are less suited to cycling, and the Australian outback is so vast and challenging that driving is the best option, allowing you to experience the mind-boggling space of the interior. So hire a camper van, or buy a second-hand vehicle and then sell it on once you finish your driving tour. You will have the freedom to explore the diverse Australian landscape on the one million kilometres of road that span the country. Try the 931-km adventure along the coast and past the Great Barrier Reef from Cairns to Brisbane, and then head on further through Hunter Valley and past Coffs Harbour to the Gold Coast. You could finish your trip with a trek inland to admire Ayers Rock and Alice Springs. Bear in mind that you will need an International Driving Permit (IDP) to drive abroad.

INTER-RAILING

This classic way of exploring Europe is just as popular as ever and now permits even more extensive travel, allowing you to visit countries across Eastern and Western Europe and North Africa. It even includes ferry passage to the islands of the Mediterranean. If you opt for all the zones, a whirlwind tour of 29 countries in 30 days will make it a great taster trip of Europe. Otherwise you could just choose your favourite locations and spend more time in each – tailor it to suit your needs. The Inter-Rail pass offers you incredible freedom and you don't have to be under 26 years of age to benefit. Save money on accommodation by choosing overnight journeys. You're guaranteed to make new friends along the way.

WALK THE GREAT WALL

Stretching across the mountains of northern China, from Gansu Province in the west to the mouth of the Yalu River in the east, the 2,000-year-old Great Wall of China winds its way for 6,700 km across stony deserts, grasslands, mountain ranges and immense plateaux. Walking along it provides an excellent route for exploring China's varied landscape and history – it was originally built as a defence against the Mongols. Many people don't have time to do more than day trips from Beijing so if you devote more time to a longer trek you'll get much more out of it, visiting parts that other walkers don't reach; in many places it's daunting and challenging. If you want to go the whole hog (it would take about 300 days) or a substantial stretch, it makes sense to join one of the many fundraising treks organised by charities each year.

THELMA AND LOUISE ROAD TRIP

Hire a convertible and head off across the expanse of America with your best pal in this classic road trip from Oklahoma to Las Vegas, covering seven states. You'll take in some of America's most iconic scenery and famous routes, including the way to Amarillo, Route 66, the canyons of Utah, Dead Horse Point, Monument Valley and the Grand Canyon. In most places you can stay in motels en route; but as the journey does cover large expanses of desert, you'll want to stock up on drinking water before you set off. And make sure you've got a spare tyre. Stay safe on any clifftop roads as well.

OVERLANDING

Ideal for remote and rugged places way off the tourist trail, overlanding means travelling with up to 20 other 'overlanders' on a self-reliant, custom-made expedition truck that has everything you need, including cooking equipment, tents, a guide and, of course, a driver. Trips are often weeks or months long and you're part of the team for the duration. You stay at campsites and budget accommodation and join in with shopping at local markets, cooking and cleaning. A 15-week overland trip from Bishkek in Kyrgyzstan to Singapore, for example, will take you on a mind-blowing adventure across Central Asia following the ancient Silk Road routes, staying on the Tibetan plateau. Overlanding is about taking the road less travelled, sharing new experiences with a group, and immersing yourself in different cultures.

ONE HUMP OR TWO?

Meander on a camel safari through the spectacular desert east of the Nile towards Mount Sinai with a Bedouin guide who has expert knowledge of the terrain. Camels might be a temperamental way to travel, but they are perfectly adapted to the desert and will allow you to explore areas beyond the reach of man-made vehicles. Don't forget your sunhat and shades, sunblock and a good sleeping bag to keep you warm at night. The camels ridden in North Africa and the Middle East are the more common one-humped variety. The Gobi desert in Mongolia is one of the few places that you can take a ride nestling comfortably between the two humps of the rarer Bactrian camel.

FLYING ADVENTURES

Humanity has longed to soar like a bird since the beginning of history, and every year thousands of people jump from planes, mountains and tall buildings seeking the thrill of flying. If you've got a head for heights, these flying adventures might be for you. And the world will never look quite the same again. Be sure to check that your insurance policy covers it, and don't forget to empty your pockets.

HANG-GLIDING

Some say hang-gliding is the closest you can come to having wings, and it's certainly one way to fly without an engine. Once you're suspended from your glider in a harness, the objective is to stay airborne on lifting currents of air for as long as possible. There's nowhere better to gain your first taste of free flight than Kitty Hawk in North Carolina's Outer Banks, home of the Wright brothers' first successful flight. Acclimatise to the apparatus by launching yourself from the top of enormous sand dunes, then get towed up by an ultralight plane and released from 600 metres in tandem with your guide. Rent one of the wooden beach houses for the perfect Outer Banks summer experience.

SKYDIVING

Sign up for a skydive and you will jump from an aeroplane and free-fall, finally opening your parachute in just enough time to slow your descent before you reach the ground. Your tandem instructor will do all the hard work, allowing you to enjoy the 200-kmph flight of your life. However, you do need to be able to keep a cool head and make sure you are comfortable with all aspects of your training before heading

up in the plane. It's one of the most popular, most thrilling gap year activities to test your nerve. For the ultimate skydiving experience, New Zealand is a favourite destination. With breathtaking views of the Abel Tasman and Kahurangi national parks, sparkling oceans, golden beaches, the Southern Alps and the magnificent peaks of North Island, plummeting 4,000 metres has never been so beautiful. If you don't fancy free-falling, you could opt instead for a parachute jump, during which you will jump from a relatively low altitude and deploy your parachute almost as soon as you leave the plane.

PARAGLIDING

Made famous by the likes of James Bond, paragliding involves jumping from a mountain suspended from a specially designed parachute, directing yourself along thermal undercurrents through the use of directional pull-strings. The easiest and safest way to gain your first taste of free flight is in a tandem flight with a qualified pilot. Paragliders are portable and easier to learn to fly than hang-gliders, and once you gain the confidence to brave the skies alone you will feel an enormous rush of freedom, although you will need to be strong. With beautiful views of the Pacific Ocean from its high cliffs, Miraflores in Lima, Peru, is an excellent place to start. Portugal also has some amazing hang-gliding sites for all levels of ability, just a half-hour drive from Lisbon, with good conditions for most of the year and the largest number of flyable days in Europe.

BUNGEE JUMPING

Some people throw themselves off buildings and bridges with nothing more than an industrial-sized rubber band attached to their feet. India might sound like an unusual place to do it, but the country has been catching up on adventure sports. Rishikesh has the highest bungee jumping platform at 83 metres (if that doesn't sound bad, just think – it's equivalent to jumping from a 22-storey building) surrounded by forest-covered mountains and overlooking a tributary of the Ganges at Mohanchatti village. Alternatively there's a nice soft option of 25 metres at Anjuna Beach, Goa. To push your fears to the limit, take a leap of faith off the Bloukrans River Bridge in the heart of South Africa's Garden Route. At 216 metres, it's the highest commercial bungee jump in the world.

MAGNIFICENT FLYING MACHINES

Imagine being encased in a part-plane, part-rocket machine as it hurtles around in a circle, suspended by a steel cable over a deep canyon. If this sounds like your cup of tea, you can 'fly by wire' at Queenstown, New Zealand. You determine your speed and height by choosing at what point to launch as you are winched slowly into an almost vertical position high above the

canyon floor. The throttle and steering controls allow you to swoop and dive and as the craft is firmly attached to a crane you cannot fly out of control at any time. This bizarre experience is the next best thing to flying a fighter jet. A similar type of experience is known as 'jungle swinging' in the hills around Cairns, Australia: believe it or not, it has nothing to do with Tarzan. You and up to two of your mates can be strapped face down into a hang-gliding harness or 'Minjin jungle swing' which is suspended from a steel cable, then you're zoomed through the jungle from a height of 45 metres to as low as one metre from the ground in 3.5 seconds, at up to 120 kmph.

BASE JUMPING

BASE jumping is the ultimate extreme sport and is only recommended for the most experienced extreme sport enthusiasts and thrill seekers. It's actually illegal in some countries, so if you do risk it, you may well invalidate your insurance policy. It essentially involves jumping off a tall structure, freefalling and then releasing your parachute at the very last possible moment. BASE stands for the four main points from which you can jump: Building, Antenna, Span (or bridge) and Earth (or cliff). To qualify for a 'BASE number' you would need to do a jump from each of these. Norway is the BASE jumping capital of Europe.

SPIRITUAL ADVENTURES

Are you seeking another kind of fulfilment – one that comes from pondering the meaning of life and perhaps discussing it with others? Experience a personal adventure with a difference by going on a pilgrimage or retreat. Discovering powerful spiritual rituals and traditions can be mind-expanding and moving in a way that will last a lifetime. You don't have to be religious – just leave your preconceptions at home, and approach new places and experiences with respect and a genuine spirit of enquiry.

WALK ST OLAV'S WAY

Stretching about 640 km from Oslo to Trondheim, St Olav's Way is the longest pilgrim route in Norway, allowing walkers to enjoy the challenges and beauty of some spectacular natural scenery. Dating back to 1031 AD, this ancient trail follows the route of the early Norse pilgrims to Nidaros, where they travelled to pray at the resting place of King Olav, who was made a saint for bringing Christianity to the land. Walk the path that pilgrims have followed for the last 500 years, alongside Lake Mjøsa, through the dense pine forests, past Bronze Age settlements and over the tundra, ending your journey at the crystal-clear waters of the fjord. Whichever section of path you choose and however you tackle it, alone or with friends, this historic and wild pilgrimage route will offer you an opportunity for an inner journey too.

LEARN YOGA FROM THE MASTERS

The ancient discipline of yoga was developed with the aim of stimulating the mind and allowing spiritual and personal development. But of course it brings physical benefits too. The breathing and meditation exercises relax the mind, allowing you to achieve inner harmony while the asanas, or postures, develop your strength, stamina and flexibility. You could book yourself on one of the many courses running at yoga centres in India where you can learn from the masters. Follow the techniques as they have been handed down through the ages in peaceful and picturesque surroundings. At the end of your stay you are guaranteed to leave feeling refreshed and ready to take on the world again.

BUDDHIST RETREAT

If you have ever wondered what it might be like to live the secluded and contemplative life of a Tibetan Buddhist monk, you could spend time on a Buddhist retreat in the mountains of the Himalayas overlooking the Kathmandu Valley in Nepal. Over the centuries, countless monks, mystics and spiritual healers have taken refuge in what may be the birthplace of meditation: the majestic Himalayas have an incomparable spiritual history and mystique. You don't have to be a Buddhist – an interest in learning about this way of life and a desire to seek peace and

enlightenment is enough. You can stay at a Buddhist monastery, sharing their vegetarian meals and learning the basics of meditation from ten days up to a month. If you prefer to combine the spiritual experience with a journey, you could go on a pilgrimage to the source of the Ganges, high in India's Himalayas. Further east, a temple stay in South Korea can include Seon (Zen) meditation, a tea ceremony and even Buddhist martial arts. Most Korean temples are ancient cultural treasures located deep in forest-covered hills.

THE PATH TO SANTIAGO

The medieval route to Santiago de Compostela in northern Spain is the most famous Christian pilgrimage still walked today – in fact, the *camino* has almost become too popular, with around 300,000 people completing it every year. There are four routes leading across France into Spain, so if you're looking for a spiritual experience it's worth choosing one of the less travelled options; there is even a Camino de Santiago on the island of Gran Canaria, a ferry ride from Tenerife, although it's not nearly as easy to follow. The most common route through Spain passes quaint villages with gothic cathedrals, and you can stay in hostels. Any route takes weeks, but the sense of achievement as you finally enter the cathedral of Santiago is well worth the effort. Plus, Santiago in Galicia is a lively university town with great seafood and a May *feria*.

TRANCE DANCE

Shamanic or trance dance is an exploration of the relationships between nature and human life that is a part of many ancient cultures. The dance teaches you how to communicate with your own 'body intelligence' through sound, rhythm and breathing exercises. You can learn and participate in the ancient tradition of shamanic dancing in Kalani, Hawaii. To help you truly feel at one with nature, indulge yourself with a water massage from a spiritual healer at the volcanically heated Warm Pond or take a natural sauna at the Steam Vents. These cracks in the Earth, created by earthquakes and volcanic eruptions, release steam heated by the Earth's core.

THE CHANGING COLOURS OF ULURU

Uluru, the giant sandstone rock in the middle of Australia also known as Ayers Rock, can be called the country's spiritual heart, and thousands of tourists visit this astonishing monolith every year. The rock is sacred to Aboriginal Australians and central to their myths and legends about the creation of the land. As one of their 'dreamtime' tracks lies across the climbing route, the Aboriginals would really prefer that you didn't attempt to climb it. Instead, sit back and soak up the natural energy forces of 'Tjukurpa', which Aboriginals believe spring from a hollow in the ground beneath the rock. The best time to view this moving spectacle is at sunrise, when the rock's colours shift from blue to violet to glowing red. Various outcrops represent ancestral spirits, and the Aboriginal tribes of the area still use Uluru for their rituals.

WEIRD AND WONDERFUL ADVENTURES

Been there, done that, got the T-shirt? Think you've seen it all? Think again. These unusual and exciting adventures prove that there's always another new experience around the corner. Here's your chance to try something your fellow backpackers might not have thought of...

SANDBOARDING

Sandboarding is snowboarding without the cold and the ski-lifts. As you glide down sparkling sand dunes at top speed in a desert or by the coast, feeling sheer thrill and exhilaration, you also get to enjoy the warm sunshine. Anyone can try it, and the better you get, the bigger the dune you can tackle. Dry sand dunes yield the best results: avoid boarding on areas covered by dune grass, as this fragile element of dune ecology is vital to their existence. It's also a good idea to wear a helmet in case of hidden rocks and driftwood. Have a go at this fun sport at Cape Town's Betty's Bay, in the Sahara or Namibia. The US has too many locations to mention, and Brazil also has great spots all down the coast, such as Fortaleza in the north and Florianópolis near São Paulo in the south.

BOULDERING

If you enjoy the challenges of climbing but are a little overwhelmed by dizzying heights, you could opt for bouldering instead. This sport allows you the freedom of climbing without the use of ropes and harnesses, putting your climbing skills to the test by tackling short distances up rocky outcrops and isolated boulders. Some of the best bouldering terrain is to be found in the USA in Arizona and in Yosemite National Park, California. Bouldering enthusiasts who would like to pit their talents against others could take part in the Phoenix Boulder Blast in Arizona. Over 600 competitors take part in this three-day festival of climbing fun every April; it's an excellent place to swap bouldering stories around the campfire at night.

WADI BASHING

Wadi bashing involves taking a 4x4 out into the desert and driving along the twisting paths of dry, rocky riverbeds. Driving along wadis is fairly undemanding, but driving over sand can be tricky: a good way to maintain traction in soft sand is to ensure the tyres are deflated to between half and two-thirds of road pressure; not too much in case the wheels get damaged. If you take your camping gear you could also enjoy

an overnight stay in the desert. But if you're not actually planning a night in the desert, take a compass and a map as it's easy to get lost, as well as a jack, spare wheel, tow rope and planks of wood in case you get stuck in the sand. Fossil Rock, along the Sharjah-Al Dhaid route in Dubai, is a popular area for desert exploration, and you will find many rental companies here that will lease you a vehicle specifically designed for rattling around in. Oman's Wahiba Sands also offers wadi bashing and dune bashing. After scrambling across big piles of sand all day, watch the sun set on the extraordinary silent desert landscape.

YES I CANYON!

Navigating canyons and waterfalls using a combination of ropes, teamwork and mini-canoes can take you out of your comfort zone and offer thrill therapy galore. You'll be descending treacherous, slippery surfaces and abseiling in cold and wet conditions, but canyoning is, believe it or not, a fun and unique way of exploring hidden and otherwise inaccessible natural wonders. The canyons of the Blue Mountains and Wollemi region of Australia can stretch from 2 to 20 metres across, and

some are over 100 metres deep, which means the canyon floors only receive sunlight for just a few minutes each day. It's a good idea to have some previous experience of abseiling and/or canoeing, but organisers cater for all levels of experience and fitness, ensuring you have the right equipment and giving you the know-how to avoid hypothermia. Another breathtaking place for this is the Cordillera Blanca Range in Peru, where you can rappel down waterfalls created from snow and ice melting high above in the mountains. Or you can go canyoning down tropical waterfalls in Costa Rica. You'll learn the art of rappelling then enjoy pristine swimming holes before heading back to base feeling exhilarated.

TAKE A DIP IN THE BLUE LAGOON

Bathe in aquamarine waters heated to 37°C, surrounded by snow and lava fields in the atmospheric setting of Iceland's rugged volcanic landscape. It's hard to believe that this magical lagoon is really just a man-made feature, created by run-off from the Svartsengi power plant. Geothermal water is pumped from a mile below the surface, where freshwater and seawater combine at extreme temperatures;

it's used to create electricity inside the plant and supply local communities, and then let out (still perfectly clean) into the lagoon. The active natural contents of this unique geothermal lake will take the stress and strain from your travel-weary limbs. You can get treatments such as water massages from the spa centre and there are floating bars in the lagoon, so there's no need to leave the water when you get thirsty. The lagoon, which is located in Grindavik, is easily accessible by a 40-minute bus ride from Reykjavik; and if you want to extend your stay there are guesthouses at the lakeside. The water is actually milky-white and it's the sun that makes it look a startling shade of blue. Remove jewellery and bring your sunnies!

ZORBING

The ever-creative Kiwis always seem to be searching for the wildest and wackiest pastimes. Zorbing involves hurtling downhill at 80 kmph in a gigantic plastic hamster ball, separated from the ground by only a metre of cushioning air. Other variants include liquidzorbing, where two or three buckets of water are added to the mix and hydro-zorbing where you are left to flail about in your zorb on the surface of a lake or swimming pool. Do practise safe zorbing, though – it did prove fatal to one unfortunate person on a Russian snow slope. Zorbing has safely travelled around the world to the UK and Ireland, but one of the best places to try it is in the country it was invented, at the Bay of Islands to the north of Paihia and at Rotorua.

GO WWOOFING

This does not involve scaring the cat: it's actually a way of giving something back to nature and learning valuable skills at the same time by working on an organic farm (www.wwoof. net breaks down the name as 'World Wide Opportunities on Organic Farms'). There are more than 50 WWOOF groups all over the world and usually you work for four to six hours a day, helping out on the farm in return for bed and board and an education in organic farming methods. You can expect to be involved in sowing, planting, wood-cutting, making compost or wine or cheese, harvesting, milking and feeding animals – to name but a few activities – so it's important that you embrace physical labour and demanding tasks.

NORTHERN LIGHTS AND DARK SKIES

This unique and mesmerising light show will cost you nothing and comes with nature's compliments. The auroras borealis and australis, or Northern and Southern Lights, occur close to the north and south poles of the Earth. Clouds of high-energy charged particles start to glow red, green, blue and violet as they collide with gases in the Earth's atmosphere. The Lights can be seen more vividly the further north (or south) you travel, and the further away from any nearby light source. Visit the Yukon in Canada or

Svalbard in Norway to see the Northern Lights, and Stewart Island in New Zealand or Ushuaia in Argentina to see the more elusive Southern Lights.

If you can't make it to the ends of the Earth then try instead a 'Dark Sky' experience, viewing the night sky as far away from light pollution as possible, to see our galaxy, the Milky Way. The International Dark Sky Association recognises places around the world as sanctuaries from light pollution. A sky filled with thousands of stars is breathtaking and there are now dozens of Dark Sky Places – which is not only good for us, but good for wildlife conservation. Check out a Dark Sky Place near to you and, if you can, design a camping adventure around it.

CAVING

Descending hundreds of metres underground attached only by a rope to the world above, you tackle sheer drops and underground streams to emerge into a secret underground cavern. It may sound like a scene from *The Lord of the Rings*, but actually it's caving. If you enjoy team sports, can keep a cool head in a tight situation and want to try something a little different, caving or potholing might be for you. The 180-metre drop by abseil into the second largest chamber in the world, the Majlis Al Jinn in Oman, is an experience of a lifetime – and the abseiling skills required to make the descent can be learnt in an afternoon. For more involved exploration, try the world's largest cave systems in the Alto Ribeira State and Tourist Park (PETAR), in São Paulo state, Brazil.

RACE IN A CAMEL DERBY

Every year for the last quarter-century, the normally quiet town of Maralal in northern Kenya has come to colourful life on the second weekend in August as people gather from far and wide for the annual Camel Derby. Expert riders race 42 km to the finish in this nail-biting event. If you want to join in the mayhem you can hire your own camel and handler for a small fee, then career off down the 10-km amateur track, with the handler running behind to keep your camel on the move. Alternatively, bring your bike and join in the cycling races that happen at the same event – though there have been absolutely no instances yet of camels on bicycles. The event is organised by Yare Camel Camp, a hotel and campsite of the Samburu people, as part of their efforts towards preserving their nomadic and pastoral heritage.

NAKED TANDEM BUNGEE JUMP

Fancy a free bungee jump – free in more ways than one? On Valentine's Day weekend – because what could be more romantic? – Nanaimo on Vancouver Island, British Columbia, hosts the world's only naked bungee jump. You could even do a tandem naked jump with your partner. On this 'naked weekend' all jumps are free (though you may be asked to make a contribution to a local charity) as long as you are prepared to jump in the buff. You'll earn it: February can be very cold! Nanaimo is, incidentally, the home of the Nanaimo bar, one of Canada's most decadent desserts, and the city actually has a Nanaimo Bar Trail, which may suit your beloved better. If you're still in a romantic mood, you can cross to the other side of the island through ancient forests and take a long walk down the Long Beach.

FESTIVALS AND PARTIES

Party your way around the globe with this selection of the world's greatest gatherings and freakiest festivals. The best news is that these are just the tip of the iceberg: there are hundreds of parties out there to choose from, so we've selected just a tantalising taster.

NEW YEAR'S EVE

Stars, stripes, dazzling lights and sizzling energy, star-studded musical performances and a million party-goers: that's Times Square, New York, on New Year's Eve. Go crazy with the crowd as you watch the famous New Year's Eve Ball atop One Times Square drop 23 metres down the flagpole to mark the arrival of the new year, just as it has since 1906. Wrap up warm and be sure you're looking your best as this party is broadcast to millions worldwide. It's also a good idea to get there early to ensure you get a good spot: the square tends to fill up pretty quickly, so you wouldn't want to end up blocks away from the action.

CHINESE NEW YEAR

If you enjoy the New Year festivities so much that you can barely wait for next year's, the good news is that you don't have to. The Chinese New Year is on the first day of the lunar year, which usually falls in late January or early February, so it's perfectly timed to help banish those post-festive season blues. The celebrations in China last for 15 days and include colourful processions, dancing dragons and resplendent firework displays (the Chinese invented them, after all), culminating in the Festival of Lanterns where families light lamps to guide their ancestors to the party. The official holiday lasts three days and many people take a week or longer off work, so book in advance.

SNOW AND ICE FESTIVAL

For a trip to the real-life version of Edward Scissorhands' magical ice sculpture garden, head to Sapporo in northern Japan at the beginning of February for the Snow and Ice Festival, or Yuki Matsuri. Join the two million visitors who come to wander the streets among towering palaces, monsters and maidens, vengeful gods and demonic creatures of the underworld. The festival began spontaneously in 1950 when a group of six secondary school students built snow sculptures in Odori Park. The enthusiasm of this gesture in the bleak post-war period caught on quickly with the local people and the festival has been happening every year ever since. In 2003 over a thousand people spent a month building a scale model of the British Museum out of snow.

RIO CARNIVAL

No one knows how to party like the Brazilians. And to prove it, the already vibrant city of Rio de Janeiro comes alive every February in a succession of exuberant and colourful parties during the world-famous Rio Carnival. The highlight of the four-day event is the Samba School Parade that will have you itching to join in the dancing as thousands of sequined and feather-clad performers, on spectacular floats, strut their stuff in the Sambadrome. Alternatively, lose yourself in the street dancing that takes place all over the city. The passion and Latin spirit of it all, combined with the tropical climate, will have you partying until dawn.

HAPPY HOLI

The general aim of this vibrant day is to set off in the early hours of the morning and strike as many fellow revellers as possible with packets of brightly coloured powdered dye, or *gulal*, and coloured water bombs before midday. The ancient Hindu festival of Holi, which celebrates the coming of spring and the triumph of good over bad, is all about colours and sharing love. It takes place in the northern states of India around the time of the full moon in late February or early March. At noon the action abruptly stops and participants then head to bathtubs and rivers to rinse off and enjoy an afternoon of eating sweets and chocolate, sending messages of love and friendship, and regaling each other with tales of the morning's action.

ST PADDY'S DAY IN... TOKYO?

You don't have to be Irish to celebrate the country's patron saint on 17 March. Colonial New York City hosted the first official St Patrick's Day parade in 1762 because of the large number of Irish immigrants to the city. And it's still one of the world's most popular, with 100,000 Irishmen (actual and honorary) on a parade of marching bands that starts out on 5th Avenue at 44th Street and finishes at 86th Street. The Wearing of the Green is a big element – and so are green beers and green bagels. Chicago goes one step further by turning its river green, while Montserrat in the Caribbean also has strong Irish heritage so you can listen to steel drums as you wear green with pride. Most surprising, though, is the dedication of the Japanese to celebrating St Patrick's Day all over the country.

TAMING THE SNAKES

On the first Thursday in May, the tiny village of Cocullo in Italy is awoken by fireworks. A statue of St Domenico is then draped with snakes and carried by men through the streets. This is one of the most bizarre processions you will see – but even more bizarre is the fact that hundreds of snakes are captured two months earlier on St Joseph's Day (19 March) by villagers from the surrounding hills of Abruzzo. This practice started back in 700 BC, when Abruzzo was so infested by snakes that the local shepherds asked for Apollo's help. After a noisy procession to the edge of the village, the creatures are released back into the wild. The villagers believe that this tradition of 'taming the snakes' protects them from snakebites for the rest of the year.

SPRING BREAK

If you think that Spring Break is just one big frenzied beach party for students then you're right. It's also a time-honoured tradition in which university students congregate to party like mad before their finals. With miles of sandy beaches, perfect weather and great clubs, Daytona in Florida is the place to join in this hedonistic ritual. Bring your sunscreen and your flip-flops and prepare your best party piece for the festivities that take place around the last two weeks of March every year.

DRAGON BOAT FESTIVAL

On the fifth day of the fifth lunar month throughout China you can munch on *zong zi*, or stuffed rice balls, and watch the dragons go by as the Chinese people honour Qu Yuan. This celebrated poet and adviser to the Zhou Emperor threw himself into the Milou river when he realised the Zhou had been defeated, and fishermen rushed out in their long boats to throw rice to the fish to stop them from eating his body. The celebrations take the form of boat races, in long canoes shaped like dragons. Before they set off down the river there is a special ceremony where eyes are painted on the boats to bring them to life. You can join in with the races or sit back and watch the spectacle. And apparently if you can make an egg stand upright at exactly noon, you'll have good luck for the rest of the year.

MIDSUMMER SOLSTICE

The summer solstice is the longest day of the year, and in much of Sweden the sun barely sets at all, so head there to be part of one of the world's biggest solstice celebrations. In this country where summers are short, it's a public holiday and on the third weekend in June everyone escapes to the country to make the most of the midsummer weather, with flowers, maypoles, dancing and all-night parties. Sample some delicious midsummer fare including fresh potatoes with pickled herring and the first strawberries of the season, all washed down with schnapps. The open-air museum in Skansen, easily accessible by bus from Stockholm, hosts a three-day celebration every year, but you will find summery happenings all over the country.

WIFE-CARRYING WORLD CHAMPIONSHIPS

Wife-carrying is known as *eukonkanto* in Finnish and it originated, according to legend, when a group of nineteenth-century outlaws took to carrying women away along with other spoils. Nowadays, wives volunteer to be carried in this popular foot race in Sonkajärvi, held every July and attracting a great international crowd – especially since the first prize is the wife's weight in beer. Competitors run a distance of some 250 metres, tackling log hurdles and a water obstacle (which presents the biggest problem for the wife when being carried upside down). Oh, and just so you know, it's not essential to carry your own wife. Qualifying events take place from Estonia to Hong Kong and, according to officials, you can incorporate training into your everyday life.

RIDE 'EM, COWBOY

Catch 'The Greatest Outdoor Show on Earth' in Calgary when the town transforms into a living celebration of cowboy culture for the Stampede in July. Starting with a spectacular parade, the party includes just about every western-themed event you could imagine. Watch buckin' broncos at the rodeo or settle in for an evening of entertainment at The Grandstand Show, which includes chuckwagon rides and live country music. If you want to join in with the spirit of the Stampede, you have to dress western. Cowgirls, learn from local experts how to stampede in style: mix your own look with one or two rodeo-type accessories, e.g. cowboy boots with a sundress or denim cut-offs. Fellas, don't forget your boot-cut jeans, a shirt with snap buttons, and obviously a cowboy hat.

MUD FESTIVAL

Slip on your swimwear, so to speak, and head to Boryeong in the South Chungcheong province of South Korea for a week of slithery fun in this crazy festival that takes place every July. Boryeong boasts almost ten million square metres of mud – and that's not something most places would boast, which tells you a little bit about the kind of place Boryeong is. The gloop is famed for its cleansing and healing properties, and during the festival there is an endless array of ways to enjoy it. From mud baths and massages to mud wrestling and mud slides, this festival has it all. You can try your hand at mud body painting or make an entry in the mud sculpting contest if you're feeling creative.

YOU SAY TOMATO, I SAY LA TOMATINA

Some 20,000 people arrive in Buñol, near Valencia, on the last Wednesday of August to paint the town red. But their modus operandi involves truckloads of squishy tomatoes. First, everyone gets hosed down with cold water. Then the firing of a cannon signals the beginning of an hour of intense, tomato-flinging fun. The origins of this festival are obscure (apparently something to do with a food fight in 1945) but the general idea is to throw lots of tomatoes at people. Up to 140 tonnes of the ripe fruits are brought in from surrounding farms for the occasion, which leaves the local authorities one almighty ketchup-coloured mess to clean up once the fun is over.

BURNING MAN

At Black Rock in the Nevada desert around a week before Labor Day, at the end of August or the start of September, tens of thousands of people gather for the world-renowned alternative festival of Burning Man, devoted to self-expression and creativity. A temporary art 'metropolis' springs up in the middle of the desert, and as 'citizens' you can get involved in large art installations, theme camps, body painting and naked dancing. The week culminates in the torching of a 15-metre-high wicker figure. All the pieces of art made at the festival and everything else brought to Black Rock is torched, leaving the area exactly as it was before the festivities began.

OKTOBERFEST

Beer and sausages and six million of your closest friends – sounds like your kind of party? Then Oktoberfest is, of course, the perfect festival for you. Every year, in late September or early October, masses of visitors crowd into Munich and consume five million litres of beer and over 400,000 pork sausages in the beer tents that line the streets. There is also an opening parade of the Oktoberfest landlords and brewery-owners as well as funfair rides and brass-band concerts, all generously provided by the Munich breweries. It's probably not essential to know how to order a beer in German, but you may need a dark room to recover in afterwards.

DAY OF THE DEAD

Mexicans love a fiesta, and these occasions are a great way to get up close to Mexican culture. In Oaxaca, inhabitants honour the dead in a two-day celebration that begins at noon on 1 November. Families spend the holiday at the graves of their loved ones, cooking meals, praying and recounting tales of the dead. The real celebration kicks off after sunset, with a parade towards the cemetery accompanied by skeletons on stilts and people carrying bunches of vibrantly coloured flowers. Inside the cemetery, the graves are lit with candles. Stands sell food made especially for the occasion, such as cooked cactus, waffles made in the shape of crosses, and sugar skulls. The good-humoured celebrations continue until dawn, accompanied by the scent of incense and the sound of mariachi bands.

FULL MOON PARTY

The party starts at dusk, when the moon rises over the crescent of white sand at Haad Rin Nok beach, Koh Phangan, Thailand. Once, it might have been quite romantic... Now, as thousands of lamps are lit, it's the cue for the dance frenzy to begin. This much-exalted celebration takes place every month on the night of the full moon, and it's free. Up to 10,000 people from all over the world go wild as international DJs take it in turn to blast out music (techno, trance, reggae) on over 15 different sound systems along the beach. It's easy to drift from one area to another among jugglers, fire-eaters and pyrotechnic displays, so you're sure to find something you'll like. The party keeps going until the early hours of the morning: the perfect high note to end your gap year adventures.

CHECKLIST

- ☐ Whale watching
- ☐ Wild West cattle drives
- ☐ Swimming with dolphins
- ☐ African bush walking
- ☐ Horse trekking
- ☐ Watching orangutans
- ☐ Meet mountain gorillas
- ☐ An ethical elephant experience
- ☐ Great white shark diving
- ☐ Watching the wildebeest
- ☐ Animal welfare
- ☐ In the deep (scuba diving)
- ☐ Snorkelling
- ☐ Rafting
- ☐ Paddle your own canoe
- ☐ Jet-skiing
- ☐ Sail away
- ☐ Go jump off a cliff…
- ☐ Surfing
- ☐ Windsurfing
- ☐ Kite surfing
- ☐ Spend a year doing the sport you love

- ☐ Cuisines and cultures
- ☐ Open-air opera
- ☐ Learn to tango
- ☐ The art of capoeira
- ☐ Meet indigenous Australians
- ☐ Get steamy in Hungary
- ☐ Dog-sledding
- ☐ Eat fugu
- ☐ The footsteps of artists
- ☐ Appreciate the ancient Incas
- ☐ Mountain biking in Corsica
- ☐ Rock climbing
- ☐ Via ferrata
- ☐ Albanian 'Alps' adventure
- ☐ Abseiling
- ☐ Trek Mount Kilimanjaro
- ☐ Winter in the mountains
- ☐ Heli hiking on a glacier
- ☐ Volcano walking
- ☐ Trans-Siberian railway
- ☐ Hostel hopping

- ☐ On your bike
- ☐ On the road
- ☐ Inter-railing
- ☐ Walk the Great Wall
- ☐ *Thelma and Louise* road trip
- ☐ Overlanding
- ☐ One hump or two?
- ☐ Hang-gliding
- ☐ Skydiving
- ☐ Paragliding
- ☐ Bungee jumping
- ☐ Magnificent flying machines
- ☐ BASE Jumping
- ☐ Walk St Olav's Way
- ☐ Learn yoga from the masters
- ☐ Buddhist retreat
- ☐ The path to Santiago
- ☐ Trance dance
- ☐ The changing colours of Uluru
- ☐ Sandboarding
- ☐ Bouldering
- ☐ Wadi bashing
- ☐ Yes I canyon!
- ☐ Take a dip in the blue lagoon
- ☐ Zorbing
- ☐ Go WWOOFing
- ☐ Northern lights and dark skies
- ☐ Caving
- ☐ Race in a camel derby
- ☐ Naked tandem bungee jump
- ☐ New Year's Eve
- ☐ Chinese New Year
- ☐ Snow and ice festival
- ☐ Rio Carnival
- ☐ Happy Holi
- ☐ St Paddy's Day in… Tokyo?
- ☐ Taming the snakes
- ☐ Spring break
- ☐ Dragon boat festival
- ☐ Midsummer solstice
- ☐ Wife-carrying world championships
- ☐ Ride 'em, cowboy
- ☐ Mud festival
- ☐ You say tomato, I say La Tomatina
- ☐ Burning Man
- ☐ Oktoberfest
- ☐ Day of the Dead
- ☐ Full moon party

MUSIC
FESTIVALS

AN ESSENTIAL

pocket guide

TO SURVIVING

in STYLE

Tamsin King

MUSIC FESTIVALS

An Essential Pocket Guide to Surviving in Style

Tamsin King

Paperback   ISBN: 978 1 84953 701 8   £5.99

Tips and ideas from transport to
tents and style to scrimping.

Festivals come in every shape and size, but what unites them is that they are a wonderful opportunity to get away from daily life and have an awesome party! This guide is packed with tips to help you make the most of your festival experience, whether it's at a sprawling tent city or a small but perfectly curated boutique festival.

HOW TO SURVIVE UNIVERSITY

an essential

POCKET GUIDE

Tamsin King

GAP YEAR ADVENTURES

First published in 2006
This revised edition copyright © Summersdale Publishers Ltd, 2016

Research by Lucy York and Jennifer Barclay

Summersdale Publishers Ltd
46 West Street
Chichester
West Sussex
PO19 1RP
UK

www.summersdale.com

Printed and bound in Malta

ISBN: 978-1-84953-954-8

Substantial discounts on bulk quantities of Summersdale books are available to corporations, professional associations and other organisations. For details contact general enquiries: telephone: +44 (0) 1243 771107, fax: +44 (0) 1243 786300 or email: enquiries@summersdale.com.

Disclaimer: The publisher cannot be held responsible for any loss or claim arising out of the use, or misuse, of the suggestions made herein. Please take all necessary precautions and seek the advice of qualified professionals when engaging in potentially dangerous activities.

GAP YEAR ADVENTURES

AN ESSENTIAL *pocket guide* TO MAKING *it* COUNT

Tamsin King

summersdale